Angst, Anxiety, and Acceptance

a relatable guide to a teenager's life

Kimaya Saijpal

ISBN 978-1-61431-076-1

Design and Layout: Val Sherer, Personalized Publishing Services

To the people who want to achieve,
and still dare to dream.

Preface

Society has royally screwed over every single one of us. We are expected to be 'everyone's' type. Skinny, yet curvy, but if you're too curvy then you're fat. If you're too skinny, you're anorexic. And of course, if you don't excel in all the possible subjects you take, you're stupid. We are expected to be perfect at everything we do, and the second we show weakness, we are immediately pounced on by all that are close to us. We are all judged for what we are not, and rarely praise for what we have: our skills, our intelligence, our individuality. It's up to every single one of us to praise each other for what we have, and not bring down others for what they are working on. We are all on our individual journey to being the best person that we possibly can, and for some of us, it can be scary getting through our day to day lives because we feel like we're alone in life. Trust me, you're not alone. I started writing as a way to show the people in *my* life that they are not alone, and that everyone all over the globe is just waiting for someone to tell them that "where you are in your life is completely ok." Well, here it is. This is my way of telling you that your journey is *your* journey. Here are stories that have shaped me into the person that I am today, and I hope that these will inspire you to convey your own unique stories, in the ways that you excel in. Write a song, write a book, make a piece of art.

But *make* your story heard. It's these stories that leave the greatest impacts on others, and it's this notion that pushes society further into the future.

Contents

Brace Yourself

Memory is an interesting thing. Two people can go through the same experience, and still have different thoughts and feelings associated with the event. Sometimes, you'll even remember an important event in your life in a completely different way than you first thought, simply because your outlook on that aspect of life has changed. I remember one such moment, when I was 11 years old, anxiously waiting to receive news that I knew would change my life.

I recall it all so vividly. The X-ray room was dim, bleak, and filled with machinery that looked like it could have been used to rehabilitate soldiers in the Civil War. I was forced to strip down to my underwear in front of the mysterious, oddly enthusiastic woman I had just met. As I took off each layer of my clothes, the air became more and more still, and I became more and more afraid. This was the first of many of my body-related, anxiety inducing, experiences.

"Darling, today is going to be simple. I just want you to stand really still and try not to move until after I click the button," she said.

The button. This button would seal my inevitable fate. Any doubts I had about my condition would be clarified after the 37 minutes it took the X-ray to develop.

"Ok sweetie, I'm going to click the button in three, two, one." And just like that, my days of carefree joy were numbered.

Mom, Dad, and I waited in the check-up room, where the bleak walls gave no comfort, and overly perky nurses periodically rushed in to inform me that "everything will be alright." 11-year-old me saw past their fake smiles and reassuring nods; it was obvious that everything was not OK. That I was not OK. I despised them for lying to me, for giving me false hope for the sole reason of preventing a melt-down.

Not long after, Dr. Richard came in.

"Kimaya? Hello, I'm Dr. Richard, and I will be your doctor throughout your … process," Richard said grimly.

Process. That meant something *had* to be wrong.

"I'm afraid you have Idiopathic Scoliosis. We saw some misalignments of your spine in the X-ray. Together, as a team, we're going to discuss your options so that we can lessen the chance of you having to get surgery. It's good we caught it early because now you have an opportunity to wear a brace—"

"It's good?" I asked furiously. "I'm sure it's good for you. *You* don't have to wear it."

Getting fitted for a brace led to a variety of mental challenges for me. The women taking my measurements were scrutinizing all my imperfections and amplifying all of my deepest insecurities in a robotic, insensitive way, as if they didn't understand what this whole ordeal meant to me.

After a short 14 days, my brace walked through the front door, and forced itself onto the entirety of my torso. It constricted my whole body, and if that wasn't bad enough, it also forced me to wear bulky, ugly clothes.

This was during a time in my life where I had just started to express myself. Gone were the days of me wearing shirts that read "Pobody's Nerfect!" I was finally at the age where I cared about how my jeans fit, which brands I wore, and if the guy in my English class could tell that I had mascara on. I had just bought my first crop top and without even getting a chance to wear it, I was expected to replace it with extra large 'mom shirts' because of something that would cover my entire torso. I would now have to worry about the straps of my brace ripping all my favorite clothes, and for what fault of my own? I hated myself for having such a screwed up body and I hated myself even more for caring so much. I always thought I was the kind of girl who cared for more than such superficial things, but this was supposed to be the time where I found myself! Instead of being able to be the 'real me' (or whatever I thought that was), I found myself constantly tugging down my mom's old shirts, thinking that every glance was judgmental, and labeling myself "the ugliest girl alive." The sad thing is, I really felt like that for many years of my life. To this day, I have a hard time thinking of myself as more than just a girl with scoliosis, but time really does heal all wounds, and it also makes you more mature. I can still remember going into the P.E. locker room every day and changing in the restroom because I was afraid of what the other girls in my class would think if they could see *it.* If they could see what made me so disgusted, so ashamed.

The constriction of the brace also forced me to stop dancing, which was something I had done professionally since I could walk. There was too much change, and not enough time to process everything.

To make matters worse, it physically hurt to wear something so constricting. I couldn't take full breaths, and I felt a constant pressure on the left side of my body.

I tried my hardest not to bring attention to any part of my body that might give away what was wrong with me, but that didn't come without its own set of problems. One day, I came to school without wearing my brace because it was being reshaped, and the first thing I heard was from one of my close friends, who said, "you look so good today! Did you do something different? "Is that a new outfit?"

This confirmed my worst nightmares. I always knew that my brace was noticeable by anyone who looked at me, but I would tell myself that no one *really* noticed. That no one *really* cared. I knew my friend meant well, and *was* probably talking about the new outfit that I did happen to be wearing, but it just made me feel terrible about myself.

Things kept getting worse, I kept getting more anxious, and honestly, I stopped being a good friend. I was unable to see past myself, always looking for validation, always asking "I'm pretty, right?" instead of "How are you doing today?" or "Am I a good friend?" I became so superficial that I forgot that there was more to life than my condition. That being someone who people want to be around is better than being something good to look at. My priorities were so off, and they were just getting more and more off track.

Then, one day, my perspective changed. It was the middle of English class, and a book fell on my torso, and made a loud, jarring sound similar to a bang on a wooden desk. I stood in shock, ashamed that I had given people another reason to look at me differently. My face turned red, and on the verge of tears I looked around, praying that no one had heard, even though I knew that they had. Wincing, I raised my hand, getting ready to ask to leave the room. But then, someone who I didn't know very well, said, "Wow, Kimaya! You've got some really rock-hard abs!" I was shocked. Rock hard abs?

The class laughed, and I did too. That remark made me think about my brace in a more positive and comedic way. Everything my nurses, doctors, and parents had said to me finally started to make sense. I *was* lucky that we caught my condition early. I had saved myself years of back pain and surgery, in exchange for wearing a brace for a measly three years of my life.

After that event, I didn't actively try to hide my brace, I just let it be an important part of my history. I found myself becoming more open with the people close to me, and people I didn't know very well. I stopped hiding in the bathroom to change, and instead I asked the people around me to help me put on my brace. They obliged, happy to help.

I never realized that more than half the problem was my constant self-deprecation, and if I could learn to love this part of me, then no one's opinion could stand in my way. The more I didn't care, the more I noticed that others were too focused on themselves to spend much time on what I did or how I looked. As long as I was smiling and waving at my teachers and friends, they would reciprocate. The reason is simple: humans are masters at picking up on emotional atmospheres and mirroring those feelings. We all think that every dirty look is directed to us, that every glare is because of us. But we don't see the mirror behind us, and we don't realize that both of us are looking and judging ourselves. That most of those dirty looks are not for us. That dirty look is because she saw that she had spinach stuck in her teeth. She's too busy worrying about that to care about my brace, let alone talk badly about it. He's too self-conscious about his old shoes to care. Once we understand this, the answer is simple. Love yourself for who you are, and who you want to be.

I've taken a long time trying to answer the question "What does perfect mean?" I've come to the conclusion that "perfect" comes from total acceptance. There is no "perfect" because everything on this planet is unique and it would be foolish to say that we can objectively come up with an answer to that question.

Now, it would be a lie to say that I don't catch myself judging anything I think isn't "perfect": my nose, my uneven complexion, or my weight. But I try to remind myself that even the most beautiful model has insecurities, and that there really is so much more to life than how I look. When I die, I want to have impacted as many people as I possibly can. I want to have spread love, and to feel positivity radiating around me. That is what I want.

All my thoughts and memories associated with Scoliosis encouraged me to embrace my experience as part of who I am instead of disregarding it as a flaw. And the moment that once seemed like a path to eternal misery has now become a beautiful moon-lit hike with victory as its destination.

The First Time

I remember the feeling like it was yesterday. It was an unfamiliar feeling. Uneasiness, and a tight unexplainable tension in my stomach. But I shrugged it off, blaming it on nausea from not eating dinner the previous night. I double checked my bag for everything I'd need: a yoga mat, blanket, and a book to read if I got bored. My mom drove us over and asked me if I wanted breakfast. I said yes, even though I wasn't hungry. *Staying Alive* was playing on the radio. *How fitting.*

We drove up to the convention center with bagels in hand, and my mom gave me words of encouragement, asking me to call if I needed her. I sighed. I *was* excited, because I was going to see all of my meditation friends at the week-long camp we were doing. But that nagging feeling kept me preoccupied. I finished my bagel and walked into the room filled with 40 of the extremely hyper kids I would spend the next week with, still feeling uneasy.

Luckily, I saw many familiar faces, and as I rushed over to talk to them, my strange feeling disappeared, and I stopped thinking about it. First up on the agenda, a 'nature' walk to get to know everyone. Nature really just meant the park right next to the convention center, but we all obliged. It was the fourth of July after all, so we were obligated to have some outdoors fun. I ran inside to bring my book with me. I never considered myself an outdoors person, even if in the middle of a big city, it didn't seem all that natural. But, if push came to shove, I'd rather read my book than play baseball or tag.

We stepped outside. It was a beautiful, sunny day, and even though I was out of my comfort zone, I couldn't help but put down my book. I smelled the fresh summer air and felt a sense of release. *Strange*, I thought.

But the blue sky and the leaves from the big oak tree had my full attention. I was chosen to be leader of the sharks and minnows game, and again, I obliged. The ambiance and the fact that it was almost 100 degrees outside must have caused the change in my personality. We played and played, and I ran and ran, but ended up feeling like throwing up, so I finally stopped, sad that I wasn't able to win, but also relieved that I could go back to reading my book.

It was time for the first meditation of the day. I stepped back into the cramped room and sat down on my yoga mat. Collectively, we were all tired—the students, the volunteers and our teachers. By design, the first meditation happened to be one where we were lying down, which was the perfect remedy for almost-heatstroke. We started the meditation sitting up, with the goal to get into a state where we weren't worried about the outside world, and where we were focused on finding our inner peace. I focused on my breath, and started to giggle, despite trying my hardest to be as serious as possible. Feeling ashamed, I stifled my laugh, which only caused me to feel more uncomfortable.

Something that my teacher said stuck with me. "Let go of all judgement. Of others, of yourself. Feel what you are feeling, and don't force something to happen. Something *is* happening," Something *was* happening. At that moment, I opened my eyes, and looked down in my lap, to see my neon pink colored tights, stained with bright red spots. *Blood.* I finally realized what had been making me so nauseous, anxious, and rash. *My Period.* I thought. *It finally happened.*

I looked around at the kids next to me. All of their eyes were shut. Everyone around me was in a deep state of meditation. I was wondering why I wasn't freaking out. I had heard horror stories from my friends about it happening in school, during soccer practice, and art class, and they had perfectly reenacted how embarrassed and stressed they were about it. But something about the meditation had me in a calm and collected state. I stood up, wrapped my jacket around my waist to hide any leaking, and walked out the door, trying to find a woman that I could talk to.

I walked a few minutes before finding two women, both of whom looked like they were in their late 30s, who asked me if everything was ok. I smiled at them, and started to explain my situation. I could see the shock and amusement on their face, caused by how well I was handling my current dilemma. They called my mom, who asked if I was ok, and I told her that I was fine. She asked if I wanted to get picked up and I again said no, not wanting to cut the fun I was having short. I asked her to bring me a new pair of pants, and chatted with the two ladies, waiting for my mother.

When I look back on this day, it's funny to me how calmly I handled the situation. I think of all the things that could have gone wrong, like me screaming in the middle of the meditation, or me leaking and not knowing until someone told me. But then I realize that these moments, these events, are all stories that make us who we are. Everything we go through is a story with millions of points of view. I had taken something that most girls would freak out about and made it into a memory that I will forever recall as the first time I showed true maturity. Each one of us puts a different amount of importance on these stories, which is why I find it so interesting to tell them. You may latch on to this one, another one, or you may latch on to the feelings that this invokes. It's beautiful how different things stick with different people.

I hope that I've taken the topics I write about in this book and made them into something that you cherish and love forever, as I cherish and love this memory. Without further ado, welcome to *Angst, Anxiety, and Acceptance, a relatable guide to a teenager's life.*

home

deep breaths
they don't know
and they can't ever find out

i close my eyes
and remember holding you in the night
it was special

our untold language
the dancing
our own little world

in the beginning all secrets are exciting
but there comes a point where you can't hold it all
anymore
the hurt, the ache
my tears hurt as they roll down my cheek
and burn scars into my skin
but i try to smile
to not taint what was once ours

i remember when i knew how to fly
but that was years ago
i plead to anyone listening
"can the two of us be enough?"
i beg and beg
but i know the answer

Not What I Thought This Would Be

SARA'S PERSPECTIVE

"Abha darling! It's so good to see you. It seems like we haven't talked in ages," I said with a glimpse of irritation on my face. We had just come back from summer break, and Abha, my bffnw (best friend forever no matter what) hadn't responded to any of my texts to meet up.

Strange. It's not like she had anything better to do. We were two peas in a pod. Never angry, never divided, never apart. If Abha wanted to have fun, I should have been called. *Why didn't she call me? I sent her so many texts. Is she mad at me? She can't be mad at me, that would break our girl code. Ha, she can't be mad at me, I haven't done anything wrong.* She *is wrong for ignoring me all summer.* She *has to apologize to me. Problem solved.* I had come to the conclusion that I was not in the wrong, but wasn't too pleased with Abha.

"Hey Sarah," Abha smiled. "Sorry about being MIA. I was at an all-girls camp in Minnesota for six weeks. We weren't allowed to use our phones unless it was to call our parents, and that was only allowed once a week."

"But you could have called me when you got back. Six weeks you said? There was a good four weeks left of vacation. Why didn't you at least respond to my texts?"

"Texts? I didn't get them. Didn't I mention that I got a new phone number?" Abha replied, looking a little uneasy.

"No, you didn't. We haven't talked for almost three months. Here," I said as I took out my phone. "Put your new number in. We can catch up later. Gotta go to Spanish," I said with a melancholy smile.

As I walked to Spanish, I thought about how much Abha had changed. Her normally long hair had been cut to the ear, and she had gotten a tan. Minnesota wasn't exactly a place you'd go to get a tan. I kept thinking about how she hadn't responded to anything I had sent her. It seemed like she was hiding something in our conversation which was new to me, since we told each other everything. I wouldn't ask her what was going on. If she wanted me to know, she would have to tell me herself. Besides, the truth would have to come out eventually, since I was Abha's only good friend. It was just the two of us. That was the way it had been since kindergarten, and the way it would be forever. We didn't need anyone else.

If I can be totally honest with you, I knew that there was a girl in our class who wanted to invite Abha to her birthday party last year, but I let her know that she wasn't interested. It was in the best interest of Abha; that girl hadn't bothered to invite me. Sarah wouldn't have been able to survive a party knowing that I wouldn't be with her. I didn't like Rachel—the girl—to begin with, and I knew that if Abha found out, she would've been fine with it. She would have never wanted to go anywhere without me in the first place. As I said before, the two of us didn't need anyone.

I wonder what had changed. It had only been three months since the end of eighth grade. Yet Abha was acting so differently around me. Our vibe had changed. There were no secret handshakes or inside jokes. There were just pleasantries and other small talk that were never done between BFFs. Eighth grade had been so different ....

About one year ago

"Silence everyone! The next person to disrupt my class gets detention. Does anyone here want to pick up trash on the first day of school? I didn't think so!"

"Ms. Roles can screw off. It's the first day of school. Does she really expect us to be excited to learn after a long break? Not to mention, it's our last year in middle school. We are kings!" Sarah yelled ecstatically.

"What did I tell you Miss ... Rell?" Ms. Roles said as she looked down at the seating chart. "Detention," She pointed towards the section of the white board that listed *People with Detention*.

"Sorry Miss! Sarah was just trying to cheer me up. I was getting anxious over being the oldest in school. Sarah helped to remind me that being old doesn't just mean more responsibility, but it also involves more fun such as the end of the year promotions dance. I think that she doesn't deserve punishment since she was just trying to help me out," Abha smiled.

"Well in that case, since Ms. Rell was just trying to be helpful by distracting the entire class for *you*, you may join her in detention."

Abha silently giggled while writing her name on the board. Anything to be with Sarah. Forever and always.

"I called it," whispered Sarah. "You couldn't live without me if you tried."

Abha knew that Sarah meant to be lighthearted, but the comment really got her thinking: *Was she dependent on Sarah?* She didn't have very many friends, and the few that she did have were "hand picked" by Sarah.

"These girls are only here to secure our place in the social pyramid. Don't get too attached. Love you loads!"

Abha didn't show it, but she often thought about that moment two years ago. A list of little things had accumulated into Abha second guessing her friendship with Sarah. It's not like Abha had a relationship to compare to the one she had with Sarah. But, deep down, Abha felt like some things Sarah did weren't right. When the two of them were in the first grade, they made a set of rules called "Girl Code" (with the help of a thesaurus for "fancy" words) and made a blood promise to always follow them.

Abha's Perspective

Girl Code

By Sarah Rell and Abha Khatri

1. We solemnly promise to have each other's backs, and share each other's punishments till the end of time.
2. We swear to always be together, work as a unit, and never contradict one another.
3. We shall NEVER terminate this relationship.

Sarah took these three rules to an extreme level. In any situation, even when one of us was in the wrong, we had to stand up for one another. In the third grade, Sarah had stolen a "fancy" mechanical pencil from a classmate, and giggled to me about it. When the kid found out, he immediately accused Sarah, since she sat next to him, and had a reputation for being the class mafia. She said she hadn't stolen it and looked to me for validation.

"I didn't steal it, right?" she asked.

I was shocked! Sarah had told me an hour earlier that she had taken the boy's pencil. I didn't want to lie to him, she had in fact stolen his pencil! But as Sarah looked to me, I realized what I had to do. I didn't want to, but we *did* have a "code."

"No, she didn't. I think Mel did,"

Not only did this lie make me feel terrible, but it also made Mel, a friend of mine, stop talking to me.

This happened many times, and over the years I got used to it. I still had a nagging feeling in my head that what I was doing was wrong, but I really did love Sarah, and she was my best friend. My reason for covering up for her changed over time. When I was more morally involved, I used to say that I had sworn to always be there for her. But, as time went on, I just started getting used to it. I would be her witness, the people involved would never talk to us again, and we repeated the cycle. It got to the point where no one wanted to talk to us, because we were such horrible people.

This *hurt*. I had never wanted to be the girl that everyone avoided, the girl that no one wanted to be around. But I wasn't confrontational, and I was too timid and too scared to tell Sarah how I felt. And she wasn't all bad. When we were alone, she was funny and sweet and caring. But the second we stepped out, she would only find ways to use me.

I felt trapped in the friendship. There was no one to talk to (other than Sarah, of course) and I was in the wrong. Sarah could always tell me what to do, but it came down to *my* actions. I had lied. I had hurt a lot of people. I couldn't just come back from that.

The day Sarah told me that I couldn't live without her was the day that everything clicked into place. It was true. Without Sarah, I would have no friends, no status, no life. I didn't want to be like someone who couldn't breathe without someone pressing on their lungs. That was the day I promised to become my own person. To become a person, I could look in the mirror without shame. I didn't want to have to worry about being late to something and upsetting Sarah, or the fact that I hadn't bought the snack that she liked.

"*You can't live without me if you tried.*" What I wanted to say was "Yes I can! I am not your slave! I am your equal. You need to start treating me like you would someone you respect, not just someone you know can do things for you. I feel very hurt. I feel like I've wasted ten years of my life!"

Of course, I was too timid to say that. But from that day on, I gradually spoke my mind and told Sarah off when I didn't like what she did. I was still friends with her of course, but I think we both felt the friendship coming to an end.

The rest of eighth grade was a blur. Sarah and Abha ate lunch together, but that was where the interaction stopped. Abha was mysteriously "moved" to the other side of Ms. Rell's class, and so the two didn't have much time to talk during school hours. Abha was always busy, and Sarah assumed that she was having "family issues." Because there was no way that Abha would choose to ignore Sarah, right?

Life was pretty smooth for Abha. She had cut all negativity (including Sarah) out of her life without making her suspicious, which gave her the chance to meet new people and go to new places, but she always felt like she was missing something. *Sarah.* They had been friends for 10 years; it would be hard to forget her just like that. Abha felt like in order for her to move on, she needed closure. She needed to tell Sarah the whole truth, once and for all. Only then would she be able to truly move on. But, frankly, she was afraid of what Sarah would do. Sarah was very possessive of Abha and would surely freak out when she found out that not only did Abha have new friends, but that she wanted to end their 10 year friendship. But it had to be done. Only then would Abha be able to be her own person.

Abha decided that she would tell Sarah at the beginning of ninth grade, so that she could start high school without any drama.

9TH GRADE, PRESENT DAY

"Sarah! I have to tell you something," Abha said as she ran towards Sarah.

"Oh, now you want to talk to me?"

"Sarah. I don't think I can do this anymore."

"Do what?"

"This. This relationship where you constantly make me feel guilty and force me to do things your way. I'm my own person. I have new friends, and I feel like I can't be my true self until I have closure with you."

"What are you saying?"

"I'm saying that I don't think I want to be friends with you anymore. I'm sure you've noticed me keeping my distance. I don't hate you, but I don't want to be the girl that everyone hates. It's just not me. I hope you understand."

"Understand? This is crazy! Whatever happened to "Girl Code?" We are supposed to be friends forever no matter what." Sarah said as tears fell down her face. "I'll do better. I'll be better. You can be friends with other people. I'll allow it—"

"See that's where you're wrong. You shouldn't have to allow me to do anything. I should be able to do things on my own account, without you making me feel guilty. I'm sorry, but I think the best thing for us right now is space. Take some time to self-reflect and I'll do the same. And don't *ever* use Girl Code as an excuse. We made it as kids, and never adapted it to our needs. To my needs."

"But this is all happening so suddenly!"

"No, this has been a long time coming. I should have told you sooner that I didn't feel comfortable, but it was also your responsibility to make me feel like an equal in our relationship. I'm done."

The bell rang. Abha went off to her next class. Sarah stood there in the hallway, in shock. How had their relationship come to this? Sarah knew that she was hard on Abha, but Abha had never spoken up. Sarah got used to using Abha and took her for granted. Once in a while, she even made Abha do things that she knew she wouldn't like as a way to show her superiority.

"I guess … this is where I went wrong …" Sarah half mumbled between tears. She knew that her relationship with Abha was over, she could tell from that conversation. This was no ordinary fight. Sarah had finally been told off, something that should have been done long ago to prevent this build up. But Sarah learned a valuable lesson that day. She would have to do better, and be better, in order to never repeat what had happened with Abha.

From that day on, Sarah tried her hardest to not be a manipulative person. It was hard of course, and took time, but progress was made. Gradually, she got up the courage to talk to Abha. Their relationship was never the same, as they never became "friends" again, but Abha appreciated the effort that Sarah put in. Over time, Sarah and Abha lost touch, but both of them remembered the friendship that they had and the life lessons that they learned from it.

she

family is given but friends are chosen
each breath, each promise, each hello
is hope for finding the one

not *the* one,
not *the* one to whom you say "i do"
but the one you trust enough.

enough to admit when you are wrong
enough to let bygones be bygones
enough to jump without a parachute
enough

and so i say,
in a blissful state,
under the stars,
under the world,
"to whom it may concern,"
will you be my enough?

not love

do you ever wish that there was a word
a word that could explain all your emotion
all your feelings
for that one person
that special person
the one friend who gets it
gets what you're going through
and if validated, could cause the biggest hole
in your heart
but they don't. instead
they make you feel worth something
It could be a mother brother sister lover
and you just feel like saying
"love"
but love is overused and has lost its power
love has become a word used for the most meaningless connection
"love you" is said to the girls we meet on our morning jog
but somehow we think "i love you" is special?
love is overrated, don't you think?
not the feeling
the word
love

A Take on Love at First Sight (About an Earring)

She was angelic. Exquisite, fascinating, and majestic. *She* was the cause of my untimely demise. But I was thankful to *Her*, for because of *Her*, I got to experience the joys of life. It was short-lived (at its best), but it was all I could have asked for in a human life.

Because of *Her*, I was fortunate.

I was proud.

I was confident.

I was loved.

I was everything *they* wanted. I had everything *they* worked long hours to obtain. But most importantly, I had *Her*.

I remember the day I first set eyes on the sweet creature I would eventually call mine. I had just finished my shift at the unimportant job I did, in the unimportant town I lived in, in the unimportant country I had a passport for, in the unimportant world I felt neglected by.

There was a part of me that felt the need to be isolated from society. No friends, no family, no significant other. I had no desire to search for any special people in my life. After all, who could ever like *me*? Who could ever understand my likes, dislikes, my needs? I wasn't "normal." I had been told this from a very early age and it just stuck. If I wasn't normal, then no one in their right mind would want to be my friend. My lover.

I walked to my bike with my shoulders hunched over and my head down. As I walked, I untied my apron and folded it perfectly before placing it gently in my duffel bag. *Another unimportant day*, I thought. *At least I have you, my trusty duffel bag.* My army green duffel with a broken string and zipper was filled with everything I owned.

As I approached the bike, my eyes caught something shiny on the floor. *An earring.* It was a rose gold stud with a big diamond. It seemed expensive for the town that I lived in. But then again, I didn't know what the fashion was these days. Girls kept on changing what and who they liked, and I could never keep up.

I checked the time. *Six o'clock.* I looked around. There was no one in the parking lot but me. I sighed. I turned around to head back to the coffee shop that I worked at. *The Bean Shack.* In our small town of Rhyhall, Indiana, there was only one coffee shop. And I was fortunate enough to get to work there.

A few things about The Shack: It's practically the only place in town where teenagers go to do anything. Kids come to do their homework, go out on dates, or just to get out of the house. There's a burger place across the street, but no one goes there unless they're with their family. The owner "Big John" is known for saying some creepy things to kids when there are no adults around. But that's a story for another day.

Here at The Shack, there is an unlimited amount of drama and gossip. For a guy like me who doesn't have many friends, it's always fun to see a relationship unfold or some good old friendship drama. My shift is every day from three to five thirty, and I work with Jason, who's the closest thing I have to a best friend. We've known each other since we came out of the womb, since our mothers are best friends. They met at a support group for new single mothers. Jason's father had died during his mom's pregnancy and my dad had left when he found out that mom was pregnant. Yup, we were those losers. The white boys with no dads. But we got along just fine. He was a fun person to talk to, even if it was only for a few hours a day.

"Ryan, what's up? Did you leave something inside? "

"No Jason, I found something on the floor, and I don't know what to do with it."

I looked at the earring. The more I looked at it, the more I thought about who it belonged to. Such a beautiful thing could only belong to someone worthy of it. She would have to be as delicate as a flower, while still maintaining poise and perfection. She would be the Cleopatra of Ryhall, with ear-level sleek, black hair, and bangs that highlighted her oval eyes. A tan, and rouge would add to her physique, and then, this earring would come into play. *Ms. Cleopatra Ryhall had been strutting down the fashion aisle with a catwalk so powerful, that each step she took made a dent in the floor. She walked to the end of the stage, took a glance at the important people in the front, and gave them a look that would make anyone outright pass out.*

But she kept thinking about her true love, Julius Caesar, the man who was set to inherit it all.

"Ryan. Ryan! Ryan," Jason clapped his hands on me.

"Did I do it again?"

"Yeah, you did. Anyway, you should go indoors and set whatever it is you have in your hand down, and head on home."

The earring. I got so caught up, imagining the owner of it, that I forgot all about it. "Thanks. Sorry about earlier, I can't control myself when … you know."

"Ya, I know."

I have a tendency to go off into this little part of my head and spiral about an alternate life and it's definitely gotten the better of me during tests, quizzes, speeches, and family events. It can be a blessing, but also a curse. At times it seems like the best thing in the world. But then I remember the reality that I'm living in, and my life seems two times worse than it is. For every ten seconds of pleasure, there's two minutes of pain. So more of a curse really.

Cleopatra was the bomb*–

A loud sound jerked me back to reality. Jason's car engine. I sighed, and took out the keys from my back pocket, fumbled with them for a few seconds, and opened the door. I walked into The Shack and put down my duffel bag, holding the earring carefully in my hands. There was something about this earring that just intrigued me. It was so simple yet so complex; expensive and ordinary at the same time. I loved it.

As I fumbled around with it in my hand, I pleaded and prayed with all my might, that this mysterious

Cleopatra would approach The Shack, and become a part of my life.

Suddenly, I heard a loud jarring at the door. Someone was trying to get in. My heart raced. *No way.* Could it be her? Without turning around, I yelled "It's open!" shakily.

Footsteps. Closer and closer. I took a deep breath in and turned around.

It was her.

In front of me stood the world's most treasured beauty. She had shoulder-length brown hair, bangs, and was rocking an outfit that seemed to be out of "Wonder Years." Bell bottoms, brown boots, and a matching mustard shirt. She was timeless. I glanced up to her face and my eyes immediately focused on hers, hazel and sparkling, as if she was trying to tell me something. I glanced to the left and noticed something shiny. *The earring.* I quickly looked left and noticed that this Wonder Woman was missing her left earring.

"Hi," she said. "I'm–"

"Cleo," I blabbered. I couldn't stop myself. She had too much in common with *my* Cleo, it only seemed fitting for that to be her name.

"Yes? How'd you know my name?"

I was shocked. Cleo was in fact her name. The universe had to be telling me that this was my chance and that I should shoot my shot. There were too many coincidences for this to not be fate.

"It came to me in a dream," I explained as honestly as I could. *Play it cool*, I thought to myself. "I'm Ryan. Welcome to The Shack. What can I get you?"

"I'll have an Earl Grey tea with no sugar and almond milk," she said methodically as if she had said it hundreds of times, to hundreds of different baristas, in hundreds of different places.

"Almond milk? We don't have that type of fancy stuff over here. Either take milk or take nothing at all," I said with a smile, hoping that this would make Cleo laugh.

"Ok then, milk it is," she said, reciprocating my smile.

"Coming right up." I hurried to bring out the best utensils we had and show off the barista skills that I had learned over my time working here. I steeped the tea leaves in boiling hot water, and poured it into our largest mug, trying my hardest not to spill any solution. Sadly, I was unsuccessful, with big splashes of tea being the product. Panicking, I used the sleeve of my white shirt to mop up the mess. Then, I poured a little bit of milk to fill the cup to the brim and slid the finished concoction across the counter so that Chloe could give it a taste.

"Earl Grey with *normal* cow's milk," I smirked. I was curious as to what was making me this confident. I was known as the introverted, silently-judging-you teen in the back of the class, just waiting for college, for my way to leave these less-than-average brains. But for some reason, this girl, this gem, this gift, was giving me confidence that I didn't even know I had.

"Why thank you kind sir," she said with a bow and she lifted the drink up to her lips.

"So," I said, "Who are you? A weird question, I know, but it's just that I've lived in this town my whole life and I've never seen you before." *But I've dreamt of you,* I wanted to add, but I thought that was over the top.

She sipped the tea. She seemed to swallow it without too much trouble, which led me to believe that she didn't completely hate the drink.

"Oh, I'm visiting for a week or so because my father is thinking of moving us here."

Here? There was nothing that my small hometown could offer anyone with ambition. Everyone who lived here stayed here, and ended up living a life that didn't make an impact on society in any big way.

"Well lucky for you, I know this town like the back of my hand and would be glad to show it to you. If you'll let me, of course." Again, this confidence was surprising me. It was as if I was a different person. And I loved this person that I was around Cleo.

"I'm intrigued by your offer, but I think I'll pass. My cousin lives here, I don't know if you know her. Her name's Patricia, but she doesn't like anyone to know her real name. It's too 'old fashioned'. She goes by Trish."

"Yeah, I know her, but you'd be better off with me," I said with a smile.

"Boys don't give up do they? Well I think I should be on my way, I just arrived and need to unpack," she pointed to her suitcase. She raised her drink. "Do you mind if I return this mug tomorrow, it's just that I'm not done with it." She reached into her back pocket. "Oh!"

she exclaimed. "I don't have money on me right now. I'm so sorry. Can I pay you tomorrow?"

"Hey it's completely fine. Here in Ryhall, we run on an honor system. And since you're new, this ones on me."

She blushed. "Thanks. Sorry again."

I smiled. "How was the drink, by the way?"

Cleo looked me in the eyes, and I looked back, with wonder and curiosity, "Oddly sweet, even though I don't taste sugar."

In a weird way, the way she described her drink was how I felt about her. I had just met her, yet she made me feel different, as if I was drinking a sugarless ice cream milkshake. New, weird, but still exciting.

"How odd," I said.

She walked towards the door, drink still in hand. I ran to help her open the door.

She turned towards me, smiling. "It was nice to meet you Ryan. And hey, who knows, maybe I'll take you up on your offer."

I smiled as nonchalantly as I could, but with how red my face was, I'm sure the whole neighborhood was aware of how smitten I was. The door shut gently behind her, but it opened my eyes to a whole new world of possibilities. Of a future full of happiness. Of a future full of *her.* It really isn't like me to be optimistic, but in that moment, I was sure that she would be back, if not just to return the mug. I looked down near the tip jar, smiling, when my eyes caught a glimpse of the infamous earring. I would have to give it back to her. Another reason for her to return to the shop, or for me to talk to her. I looked at the clock: *half past ten.*

Shoot. It was almost past my curfew. How long had I been thinking? I quickly grabbed my duffel bag and raced out of the door, barely remembering to lock up. I ran to my bike, hopped on, and headed towards my house.

Even for a small town, my house was … small. My mom and I shared a bedroom, and the rest of the house was just a connected bath and small kitchen. But I'm still grateful for all the things that my mom had to sacrifice so that we could sustain our life. When my father left, he left with most of what my mom had, and my mom, who was four months pregnant at the time, had to figure out how to provide for herself and her soon-to-be-born son, me. But even though we faced countless struggles together, nothing would stop my mom from giving me the yelling of all yellings for not making curfew.

I glanced at my watch again: 10:47. I started pedaling faster. There was no way that I was going to make it home before 11, but that didn't mean that I wasn't going to try my hardest.

Out of breath, I opened the front door and glanced up at the clock. 11:07. I winced.

"Mom?" I whisper-shouted, part of me hoping she wouldn't hear.

"Yes, honey?"

"I'm sorry I'm late."

"Late? It's barely 11:10, don't worry about it," she said with a smile.

"Oh. That's it? No, "you're so irresponsible, how could you?""

"Ryan, I trust you. You're 16. I trust your judgment, and as long as this doesn't become a regular thing, we both don't have to make such a big deal out of this."

"Ok. Love you!" I exclaimed as I kissed my mom on the cheek and hopped into my sleeping bag, thankful for having such an understanding mother, but also worried that she would change her mind if I didn't go to sleep soon.

"Ryan! That was sweet? Who are you and what have you done with my son? What happened today? You meet a girl?"

On a normal day this type of prying would piss me off, but for today, I'd let it slide. "Kind of. I'll tell you more about it in the morning."

That was a lie; I wasn't going to tell her anything, but it would be better for both of us if she thought I was going to open up to her. And with the images of Cleo's beautiful eyes and smile, I drifted into a peaceful sleep.

School the next day was one of the most painful experiences of my life, beating when I once put my hand in a fryer because my mom told me not to (I have the scars to prove it). Every class felt pointless, because Cleo wasn't there. I was yearning to get to know her, to learn about her likes and dislikes, and have meaningful conversations with her. I knew that there was no way that she could even be here, at Indigo High School, but the closest I would get to seeing her again was finding her cousin, Trish. I had known Trish since preschool, everyone in town knew everyone, but it had been years since I'd had a class with her. I wasn't even quite sure what she looked like now, but it seemed like the appropriate time to try and find out.

"Jason! Do you know where Trish is?"

"Uh, Trish Peters? Yeah, she's in my French class, I'm pretty sure she sits on the quad during lunch."

Perfect. I smiled, "Thanks Jason! See you at work!"

Jason looked confused. "I'm glad I could help?"

I could see the look of disbelief on Jason's face and it dawned on me that I was never as energetic or excited as I was in this moment. The more I thought about it, the more I realized that I was never truly present whenever I was with Jason, or anyone, even if I wanted to be. I made a mental note to apologize for being a stupid distant friend, because let's face it, I didn't have the luxury to not care about people.

"Trish! Can I talk to you for a sec?" I tapped on her shoulder.

She turned around. "Yes. Ryan?" She looked skeptical. "To what do I owe this unusual pleasure."

Understandable. Me, the kid who never socialized with, well, anyone, was bound to throw people off with my sudden change in attitude.

"Well … Cleo. I heard she's your cousin and she's staying with you. I have to return something to her, and I was basically wondering if you would be so kind as to take me to your house?"

"Oh! Well, I could just give it to her, given, you know, I live with her," Trish said matter-of-factly.

I gave her a look of panic. "No! I mean, she also has to return something to me. It would be a lot easier if I could see—"

"Ryan. Chill. I'm just messing with you. Cleo told me *all* about you yesterday, I just couldn't believe that she was actually talking about you. I mean the way she described you seemed so … normal. I'll text you the address."

She talked about me? "Thank you. So much. You have no idea …"

"Don't mention it. But also, don't get too attached, no one knows if she's staying. And you're not exactly her type."

I wasn't going to think that far ahead. Right now, I was going to enjoy any time I got with Cleo.

I texted Jason. *Change of plans, I can't come to work, will you cover my shift?*

"Sure. Have fun ;)" *Jesus.* How'd he know.

I walked up to the door and knocked. Trish opened the door and smiled. "Cleo! There's someone for you at the door."

I looked into the house, with a smile on my face, as I saw Cleo walk down the stairs. Today she was in sweats, but she still looked as beautiful as she did the day before.

"You left this," I said, handing her the earring.

"Ohmygod! I thought I'd lost that. My dad gave me these earrings and I would have been seriously pissed if I'd never gotten it back."

She looked like she had been crying. I wonder what had made her so upset. But I was here to fix that.

"Don't worry about it."

"Your mug," she walked back into the house, "Here it is. Thanks again for the tea."

Our eyes met. I took a deep breath "Hey. So, I was wondering if I could show you around town today. If you're free of course."

"Wow I've known you for less than a day and you're already asking me out on a date. You're confident for sure."

Literally the opposite of what I was. My hands were shaking, and I was sweating in all the wrong places. "No, uh I just want to make sure that you feel welcome?"

"Sure, you do. Don't get me wrong, I think it's sweet. Meet you at The Shack at six?"

"Perfect. See you then, Cleo."

"Bye Ryan." *Yes.* I did it. But now my new problem arose. *Where would I take her? Jason.*

I opened the door to The Shack, with a grocery bag in my hand. *Almond Milk.*

"Welcome to The Shack, how may I help—oh it's you, Ryan. How'd whatever you went to do go?" Jason said with a knowing smile.

"I assume you've been talking to Trish?"

"Yup. French class is super fun now that Trish and I can make fun of your big crush on Cleo. "I give him an annoyed look. "But all we care about is that you're happy. Your new attitude is an added bonus."

"Haha, the antisocial kid likes a girl who's way out of his league. How cliché. Seriously though, thank you, for the 'support,' or whatever it is you call taunting your best friend. Now, where do you think is a good place for me to take her? Not too creepy or over the top, but also a place where it can be just the two of us."

"I think you just answered your question."

"You're right. Le Jardin it is. I'm gonna make a quick drink, and I'll be out of your hair."

I ran to the back room, and made an earl grey milk tea, with almond milk, and poured it into the mug. I added a handwritten note saying, "keep the mug, it's on me."

5:59. I was patiently waiting for Cleo and trying my hardest to not freak her out. I'd never been so fascinated with a person, a person I had only just met. I don't think that it was even Cleo that fascinated me, it was almost the lifestyle that she represented, the change that she brought. A city girl in a small town, and here I was, a guy who thought I'd never be able to leave this god-forsaken place. But with this breath of fresh air, I was starting to see the little beauties in the place I called home.

I heard the bell at the door and glanced up. There she was, and here I was, ready to take her to Le Jardin.

"Ryan," she smiled. She was wearing a beautiful black and white checkered dress and here I was, wearing my stupid jeans and a plain white tee.

"Cleo." I smiled. "I took the liberty of making you a cup of tea. With almond milk," I added.

I handed her the mug and she smiled (smiling seemed to take up most of our time together), reading the note. "So … where are you taking me?"

Le Jardin. When I wasn't trying so hard to be an absolute pain in the ass, I spent whatever free time I had at Le Jardin. It was this beautiful open-air garden right next to the lake, built by a now sixty-something man who had grown all the exotic flowers for his late wife, back in the 80s. It was perfect for my spiraling, for my never-ending train of thought. But above all, it was beautiful. Just like Cleo. It *was* private property, but so far, I had never gotten caught.

"You like nature?" I smiled. She nodded. "Then you're going to love where I'm taking you."

I really wanted to get to know her, to understand what made her tick. Otherwise, I was getting involved for no reason, with a person who I didn't know a thing about. We walked out of The Shack, and started heading towards the garden, which was a few minutes away. I took deep breaths. I wasn't going to screw this up being an awkward mess.

"So, why are you here?" I asked. *A plain and simple question.*

"Why is anyone *here? Why* do people end up where they do? Why do people feel the need to have an explanation for everything?"

I stood, baffled, not knowing how to react.

"Sorry, that was 'deep' for no reason. I think I'm cool when I answer questions with some stupid indirect answer."

It's not stupid, I wanted to tell her. But I waited for her to answer the question.

"Ok ok. I'm here because my parents are getting a divorce and my dad is planning on moving back *here*. I've lived my whole life in Chicago, so my dad thought that while they're finalizing the divorce, I should get a few days to see if I like it here. It all depends on if my dad gets custody though."

We had reached the neon sign for Le Jardin which probably hadn't been cleaned or looked at since the 80s. Only three of the letters were lit and there was ivy growing on it. I reached up to the gate and quickly unlocked it with the key that I had found when I first started coming here.

The garden itself was well kept, and I always wondered when and who took care of it because every time I came there was no one there, but everything was the same. The grass was short and mowed, making a well-lit pathway with a variety of flowers on the side. There were so many exotic ones that I didn't know the names of, but funnily enough, my favorite flowers here were the sunflowers. They're well known, but I also feel like they're unique in their own way. They're big, everyone knows about them, but not everyone has seen them in real life. And I like that, I like that everyone knows what they are but tend to overlook them.

I placed my hand on Cleo's back, and guided her to the patch of sunflowers near the end. As we walked, I looked at her face, and I could see how surprised she was.

"My God you'll never see anything like this in Chicago," She looked directly at me, the setting sun hitting her face, "This is incredible," she smiled.

We both sat down next to the sunflowers, watching the sun set.

"Cleo. I'm sorry. I'm sorry about your parents; it sucks when the life that you have is uprooted like that. I never knew my dad, so I'm not missing anything, but I can't imagine what you're going through."

"Haha," She wasn't looking at me, but neither was I. We were both here in this moment, watching the sun fall down, if only to rise the next day.

"Divorce isn't as bad as people make it out to be. I know my parents aren't happy, and it would be selfish if I wanted them to stay together for me. Life is like cement that never dries. It's supposed to be this flat, concrete thing, but there are always things that disrupt it. Footprints from strangers, leaves falling in, cracks forming. Nothing is absolute, and unfortunately, that includes my parents." There was a brief silence. "Tell me something about you. Your hopes, your dreams, what you want to do with your life."

I looked at her, and I knew what I wanted to do. I had a hope, a dream, and a way to execute it. "You know how every kid wants to be a police officer or a professional baseball player or an astronaut and there comes a time when they realize that that'll never happen? Well, my time came when I was three, when I realized that there was no way that Mom or I would ever be able to pay for a college other than Ryhall Community, and that's when I stopped dreaming. But when you're so young, you don't understand what it really means to give up on a dream. You just think that's what life is, and you move on. But I don't want to move on, I want to go to college, I want to go to a place which will give me an opportunity to make my mom's life a beautiful experience. To make something out of myself, you know?"

She was looking at me now, I could feel it. "Life can be so complex. For what? Why is it that we live in a world where kids—kids like you, Ryan—will never get the chance to make a change. I hate it, I hate that you feel like you can't do what you want. And then there are people like me, who have all the opportunity, and none of the drive. I feel like you are proof that no one has it good. We really are a world of misfits."

"Chicago isn't that far from here is it? Maybe I'll go there. And visit you."

"You don't even know if I'm staying there. I could be moving here."

"Yeah right. Even if you stay here for the rest of high school, the second you turn 18 I can bet that you'll run right back to Chicago. This garden may be beautiful but it's not practical, and neither is this town. My advice? Enjoy whatever time you have here but if you have a choice, don't give up on your dreams. This town is far from bad, but it isn't going to get you to where you want to go."

"But you don't know what I want to do."

"Trust me. Unless you want to get stuck waiting tables your whole life, Ryhall isn't the place for you. And you know what, it isn't the place for me either." The sun had completely set. But the moon and the stars were so bright, and I could see Cleo's face in a whole new light.

I leaned in and kissed her. "Thank you," I said.

"For what?"

"Perspective. I've never met anyone who wasn't born and raised here, and that suffocated me. Your perspective is what I've needed my whole life to know that there is a world beyond this town." She looked at me again, and I leaned in.

She winced, "I'm not staying you know. You're right. I was never going to stay here. You, you almost made me consider it."

I smiled grimly. She looked at her watch and started to stand up. "Thank you, Ryan. Seriously. You said that I've given you perspective, but look at what you've done for me. I'll remember this."

As she walked away, I knew that I would remember this, remember her, too. And I prayed that night, I prayed to no one in particular, but I prayed that my life would bring me to her again, bring me to the girl who changed my perspective.

four a.m.

when no one is awake
and the coffee is wearing off
thoughts become a jumble
of the person i think i am
and the person i want to be

i'm sure we've all experienced
that rush of adrenaline
where anything is possible

and it's fun, it is, i swear
it's fun to forget

it's fun to forget your day job
your student loans
your strained parental relationships

it's fun, it is, i swear, *it is*

it's fun to wonder what could have been
If it wasn't for the burden of reality

but reality is real and real is true
and the truth?
we must never forget our destiny
of fourteen-hour shifts
and throbbing feet
but we must also never forget our dreams
of idealistic skies
and being free

Healing Wounds With Music

When you wake up, what do you do? Do you put your pillow over your head, wishing with all your might that time stops, and you can continue to sleep away the burdens you have? Do you even sleep? Or are you too busy with the constant thoughts that rush in and out of your head, good and bad. Is there a part of you that feels lost, rejected by society, and damaged due to a lack of self-worth? If so, congrats. You're just like me, and every other teenager out there.

My eyes open jarringly. My horrible alarm, set to the voice of Alec Baldwin, was going off on my Alexa. "I swear to God if I hear you say 'wake up sunshine' one more time I *will* throw—!" I sigh. No matter how much I curse that alarm, I never change it. It gets the job done. If that job is to give me early onset heart disease. Another *amazing* day ahead. Getting out of bed, I take a look around. What do I have that has any value to me? Sure, I've got tons of clothes, and a countless number of necklaces and rings, but what do I have that shows who I really am? My room is spotless, with crisp white walls, striped bed sheets, and two minimalistic chairs. But that's all there is. The only decoration I have is a small *Stanford* flag in the corner next to my off-white, only-used-once desk. And that's so that every day when I wake up, I can see the only true thing that brings me joy: college. Where I'll be away from my overbearing parents. It's not like I have a choice. My mother, a.k.a. the design freak, would lose her peace of mind if I was to even put one drop of personality into my "Parisian Chic" room. I walk to my connected bathroom, and do the one thing a day that brings me joy: I don't brush. Weird, I know, but I feel like it is the only thing that I can do that goes against what my parents want. Every other thing that makes me happy is a "waste of time" to them. So, I think, hey, why don't I just brush my teeth for 30 seconds a day, instead of the recommended two minutes, to gain back the time that my parents think I'm wasting. I don't think they realize that when I grow up, all I'm going to remember is studying, studying, studying, instead of actually becoming my own person. Of course, I can't blame that solely on my parents. I'm definitely not saying I'm the perfect kid. No one is. I'm just saying that teenagers, collectively, get a bad rap.

My parents aren't the typical overbearingonlywantafourpoint0andabove-extracurricularmaniac parents. They always tell me that they just want me to do my best, but they also say that my best better get me into an Ivy league. It's almost like they're contradicting themselves every day. When I do well on a midterm, they talk about how proud they are of me, and say "see, when you put in effort, you'll really be able to go places." Then both of them will go on an hour rant about how I'm going to go to the best school, get the best Masters, have the best job, and make them so proud. What most parents don't understand is that sometimes it's best to be neutral. Because when they keep praising us for all the good things we do, it gets in our brain that they only love us at our best, and never at our worst.

I go back to my room, throw on an outfit, and run down the stairs. I see both my parents sitting at the dining table. *Oh God, I'm in trouble.*

"Hi guys!" I say with a smile. The easiest way to tell if my parents are mad with me is by running to give one of them a hug. Based on how warmly received it is, I can usually tell if I'm in trouble or not. I run towards my dad.

"Not now, Ritu. Sit." He pointed to the seat directly across from my parents. *He didn't even let me hug him. How much trouble was I in?* I looked at my mom. She had my phone face down, right in front of her. *Oh no. What did they find? Did I forget to delete swear words from my text messages? Is this about one of my guy friends? Did I get a bad grade in something? Oh God no. No. They didn't find what I think they did. Did they?*

My dad opens my phone "Ritu, what the *hell* is this?" I sigh, they found it. My Instagram account dedicated to all the musical artists I love. My secret baby, the one thing I had managed to keep from them for so long. I cringe as he scrolls through my posts where I'm pining over a wide variety of different artists and bands that I love. The Smiths, David Bowie, One Direction, Kacey Musgraves, Hozier. The list goes on and on. A wide variety from modern boy bands to rock legends with a little bit of country and folk music sprinkled in. And I'm proud of the "diversity" if that's what you want to call it. I feel like I used to be one of those snobs who would tell people that my taste in music was better than theirs. I tried to be someone I wasn't by only forcing myself to like what I thought was cool, but when I realized that I set my big ego aside I realized that *music* made me happy, not the idea of being musically superior. Now, you might be wondering, why am I so afraid of my parents finding out about my love for music? Well, it's more complicated than that. My parents already know that I'm in love with music, which is why they enroll me in guitar, piano, and singing classes. They've taken this passion as another way to get me into the best college. Which I understand. Music *is* my passion; it is what I was born to do. But sometimes being forced to do something you love takes the fun out of it.

Do you ever feel like you just want to punch something really hard? Because this is one of those moments. I remember the day when I realized that my parents were never going to truly "get what I was going through" or "have my best interest in heart" unlike what they preached on their #mytruth posts on Facebook. It's not their fault, because I know that they *want* the best for me. They're just disconnected from my generation. I want to say to my parents that "you don't know how much these people mean to me" but I can already hear the response that I'm going to get.

"You're obsessed. Do you need to see a therapist? Because you're borderline crazy with all this time that you've wasted."

"It's not wasted time!" I'll scream. But no matter how much I reason with them, it'll never be enough. That's why I give them what they want to hear. Parents want us to be honest, but the minute we open up, they make us feel guilty. And I *do* get it, that there are more important things to spend my time on. But sometimes I just want to be a kid and make my own mistakes.

Accepting the fact that I'm grounded until the end of time, I go up to my room. And I think. And think and think. I think about how my parents don't get me (congrats! I'm super unique), and I think about how mad I am that they put so much pressure on me. And then I laugh. Am I really mad at my parents for caring about me? Am I seriously pissed off with them for wanting what's best for me? How stupid is that?!

I chuckle and then I come to a realization. No one, not even Mother Teressa, is perfect. In this situation, I'm not right, and neither are my parents, but we collectively have good intentions and that's what I should care about.

I look around my room and decide that I've had enough of holding back my personality. My parents will love me for who I am, and let me make my mistakes. This isn't the first time or the last time I've been less than perfect, but they've always forgiven me, and I have to respect that. But I'm also going to let myself live. Breathe. Take in what life gives me. Being a teenager is so hard because we think we're alone. But we're not. Every single one of us feels like no one understands us and you know what? Maybe no one does. But it's up to us to help those who are making the effort and show that we appreciate them. That way there are no excuses, nothing to fall back on when we do something wrong. Being a teenager is hard, but being alone is even harder.

I go into my closet and rummage around until I find it. My big box filled with posters, postcards, and stickers, of all the things *I* love. My identity, my joy. I rummage around for push pins and immediately start to add personality to my room. I pin and pin and pin and pin until it's been hours. I look around, happy to see all the people who I love looking back at me. But something, *someone*, is missing.

"Ritu! It's time for lunch!" I already hear a softness in my mother's voice and I smile. No one is against me but myself.

I open my desk, find a family photo, and pin it up, right next to my Stanford flag. There! Now my room really is filled with all the things I love. I shut the door behind me, and run down the stairs, ready to face the music.

The Life of a Writer

Type. Type Type. Type. I sigh. There's no way this will ever see the light of day. Writing has been given to us to express our stories using language, but sometimes that language, the language that aids or craft, is our downfall. English lacks words for the nuances of life. I'd love it if I could use the Swedish word "Badruka" which perfectly explains when one is gradually getting into the pool because of the cold water, only to be tormented by impatient friends. But I don't have that luxury. That's the beauty of writing though, isn't it? I get to explain how as I inch deeper and deeper into the lake, there are shivers down my spine and I hesitate, not wanting to feel the harsh water against my hot skin. Goosebumps form as I keep edging in, and the second I feel comfortable enough to go all the way, my best friend splashes me with cold water, an abruption to my peace. So, in a way, I can thank language for being simple and challenging me to get creative. Because without challenge, there is no innovation.

judgement

boys will be boys
boys will continue
to ridicule
to rape
to destroy
everything it means to be a girl

how can i be strong?
when i can't be alone
in fear
of my safety

i won't say thank you
but i will appreciate
the impact that you've had
on how i've been raised
and how i'll raise my own

When the Mind Shuts Down

Life stresses me out. I think I have more stress than the average person, and I've been trying my hardest to deal with it. But I don't know when my anxiety is going to strike. At times I'll think about something in the future and then, bam! I'll start overthinking, overanalyzing, and freaking out. I don't know how to stop it. It's not like I'm the one who causes my anxiety. But I am also one who freaks out about not having my favorite cereal in the pantry.

When my anxiety strikes, it's almost like I have another version of myself, sitting across from me, telling me that everything is going to be alright. Here's an example:

The other day, I was doing my APUSH homework when I got to a free response question. "If Alexander Hamilton hadn't been killed by Aaron Burr, what do you think he would have added to his plan for our nation's financial system? Wrong answers only."

Wrong answers only? What does that mean? Does Mr. Ramon want something that Hamilton wouldn't do? What's the point in that? How am I supposed to know what Hamilton wouldn't do? I put my head down on the table and thought to myself, "What would Hamilton not do?" *Well, I know that Hamilton was an elitist and that he believed that rich people could do no wrong. Easy, he wouldn't allow "poor" people to take out loans out of fear of not getting the money back. But then what would my answer be? The opposite of not giving a loan is giving a loan. I guess that means that he would give loans. Wait, loans are made for poor people because then when they don't pay the money back, banks can seize everything they own. I'm so confused! I don't know what to write.*

I sit up straight, only to find my old pal, Deepika 2.0. She only shows up during my most anxiety-ridden moments.

"Everything is going to be alright Deepika. I'm sure you know what you're doing. It's not like this assignment is worth a lot of your grade. It's not like this grade determines what college you get into. It's not like this one assignment is going to affect your job, your family, your life in any shape or form. Just write something that you know Hamilton wouldn't do," Depika 2.0 said, with a tone as sarcastic as a 13-year-old girl.

"That is exactly what it means," I replied, "My life is over! You show up when I'm feeling the worst and tell me things I want to hear. But I'm smarter than that. You must be trying to make me fail! Ha, I won't let you. I'm going to write exactly what Alexander Hamilton would do. I've got a good feeling about this."

See what I mean. I'm good at reading too much into things. The thing is the second I turned in the assignment, I knew that I had done it wrong. But while I was doing the assignment, a part of me doubted what I was doing, and I let that part of me consume any common sense that was still being used. I want to achieve great things in life, but I always end up ruining something that was perfect to begin with. This leads to more stress and more anxiety, until I'm so overwhelmed that I just want everything to stop. I don't want thoughts, work, friends, anything. I just want to be by myself and myself alone. But my mind never lets me do that. Anytime I try to take a nap to cool down, my thoughts come back, and my anxiety starts to attack. It's a vicious cycle.

The next day comes around and Mr. Ramon passes back our homework. I get mine back. *C+*.

No way. I knew that I had gotten the free response wrong, but I was sure that the other 3 pages had been spot on. I checked. Everything was fine except for that one problem. I mustered up the courage to talk to him.

"Mr. Ramon, you gave me a C+ on this assignment when all that I got wrong was one of the free response questions. The homework had so many other problems, why did you mark off so much for just one of them? I'm kind of freaking out."

"Oh yes Deepika, you're talking about the one about Hamilton. The directions clearly stated to write a wrong answer. You could have written anything; this question was supposed to boost people's grades! It was a simple, fun creative assignment. However, you chose to write exactly what he was planning on doing. I don't understand. I've been lenient with you in the past, but this is a college level course. You're expected to know how to follow directions. I hate to do this, since that answer was so extensive. It was just for the wrong question."

"Thanks," I said as I trudged back to my seat. My thoughts immediately started to get to me. *How much is this going to affect my grade?* I didn't know what to do. I put my head down.

Out of the corner of my eye, I saw a poster that said, "Mindfulness Week." I was curious as to what that meant. In big bold letters it said, "Meditation and mindfulness in room C-4 on Wednesday at lunch." This poster was new, and it was a Wednesday. I had heard of the benefits of meditation but had never gotten a chance to try it. I realized that I couldn't go on with my thoughts constantly nagging me like this. Something had to change. Lunch came around and I went straight to room C-4.

"Is this where you're holding the Mindfulness thing?" I asked.

"Yes. Come in darling, we're going to start in a few minutes," said a lady in her mid-forties. "We have a small group today. I don't mind, that means I get to know each of you better!"

I looked around. There were only six kids.

"Let's start with introductions. My name is Ria and I'm going to be guiding you through a mediation today. I love ice cream and spending time with my kids. Okay, who's next?"

"I'll go!" said an over hyper 9th grader. "My name is …"

I zoned out. I was starting to doubt whether we'd ever get to the mediation part.

"And you," Ria finally said. "What's your name?"

I looked at everyone in the room. I felt like they were all judging me. I took a deep breath. "Hi. My name is Deepika. I like eating pizza and spending time with my friends?"

How cliché. I don't remember the last time I ate pizza and I definitely didn't enjoy having to be a social person. But I wanted these people to like me. I've always wanted people to like me. I double guess anything and everything, even if my "hi" was over the top. *It's not that deep,* Deepika 2.0 creeps in, *Why do you care if these people like you? It's not like* anyone *likes you, really.*

She's right. I'm a burden. Someone like me, with such a weak mentality, not able to see beyond their own mental struggle, has got to be something of a burden to people I call friends. It's not like I want to be selfish, it's not like I beg and beg to over-analyze everything. But it's a part of me, a part that affects all my relationships.

"Excellent. Now that we've gotten that out of the way, why don't we start the mediation. Everyone close your eyes and sit comfortably."

I followed her instructions. Easy enough.

"Take a deep breath in, and relax the whole body. You all are high schoolers. You have the stress of school, friends, family, and so much more. Know that you are not alone, that you are respected and loved by your family and friends, and that if this seems like the worst time of your life, there are thousands of other children just like yourself who feel the same. Take another deep breath in. Breathe out. Let any thoughts that may come to your brain, and validate them! You are a unique person with unique thoughts, and you should be thankful for all of the talents and knowledge you've been given. Relax. Don't stress. You only live once; you should enjoy every single moment of your precious life." This advice felt like a godsend. I was taking deep breaths, but they were a little too deep, and a little too short. I started hyperventilating.

"See Deepika, you're fine. Everything is fine," Deepika 2.0 said sarcastically.

She was right of course, as always. When would anything be fine? I would always find some way to self-sabotage a perfectly good moment. Still hyperventilating, I excused myself and went outside to text Astrid, the only friend who never made me feel like I was a walking time bomb, waiting to explode. I found a little corner at the end of the C wing and took out my phone. My hands were shaking. In times like this, it was almost impossible for me to text. It's not that my hands weren't working. It's that I couldn't bring myself to talk to someone, to ask for help. It was pathetic being me.

D: *Help*

A is typing

A: *I'm in a parli meeting rn. What's up? Should I meet you somewhere?*

D: *It's happening,*

It only took her seconds to respond. Astrid was used to my episodes, but I always think about how much of a burden I am on her wellbeing. I know she has problems, and we're supposed to be best friends, but I know that she doesn't tell me about her problems because she doesn't want to trigger me. So here she is, always ready to console me, and here I am willing to put her through that. I should get an award for worst friend. Still shaking, I waited for the response.

A: *Where are you*

D: *Right next to Mrs. Jefferson's classroom.*

A: *omw. Till then, here's something funny I made in multimedia;)*

A: *file attached*

I laughed, opening the file. It was a gif of Bill Clinton's face on the body of one of those buff fish from SpongeBob. Astrid's humor was so obscure, but so was mine.

In less than two minutes, Astrid was in front of me, with her arms wide open.

I broke down in tears.

"Hey, hey, hey. I'm here."

We were way past usual friendship formalities. A few years ago, someone might have told me "don't cry, you're going to be ok;" but then again, a few years ago I didn't know Astrid. After I was done crying and catching my breath, Astrid finally asked me what was wrong.

"I can't explain it. But here's the deal, right? I had seen that poster for the mindfulness thing and so I decided to try it out, but you know how I get around new people. I don't know how they feel about me and that scares me. But I was finally minding my business, you know, actually trying to meditate, but of COURSE I had to ruin it with my temperamental mentality. It's safe to say that this is why I can never try new things."

Astrid looked into my eyes with a face that could only be of someone who felt pity. I appreciated it, but also wished she looked at me as more than a person who needed saving. But who am I kidding, I *do* need someone to save me.

"You said you didn't mind the meditation part, right? That it was the thought of others judging you that freaked you out?"

"I guess?"

"Well here's what I'm thinking. Go home. Go to your room. Lock your door. And put on one of those guided meditations. That way you don't have to worry about anyone's thoughts but your own."

My thoughts *were* the ones I were worried about, but her idea wasn't a bad one.

"Ok. I'll try," I replied.

I finished the rest of the school day not really paying attention, and when the seventh period bell rang, I got out of my seat and started walking home.

Using my key to open the door, I asked if anyone was home, getting no response. *Perfect,* I thought. When I had my inevitable scheduled freak-out, my parents wouldn't be home. I already had a bad day and wasn't about to take any abuse from my parents telling me what to do and how to handle my emotions. Going to my room, I shut the door and locked it, taking Astrid's advice. For a few minutes, I marveled at my room, my safe haven. Stringed lights everywhere, and polaroids of Astrid and I, and a few of our other friends. Here, I am not a burden to anyone but myself. And it's easier to come to terms with that. I am not safe from my thoughts, but I am safe from the fear of not being liked. Sitting on my bed, I take out my phone and see a text.

D: *Here's one I found that you might like. I love you, and I love how strong you are.*

A: *open link*

The link was to a visualization meditation. *A Nice, Autumn Day.* I had told Astrid I would try. And I wanted to try. I let the meditation play, threw caution to the wind, and allowed myself to feel vulnerable.

"Imagine rowing a boat down a secluded river, and focus on all of the beautiful red leaves falling from the variety of trees around you,"

Deepika 2.0 shows up next to me, on the bed, "As if you can go two seconds without me. But don't worry, I'm here for you while you try to convince yourself that everything is fine, and I'll be here for you when you realize it isn't."

I was so fed up, so tired of this being my norm. "Everything *is* fine! Tell me one thing that is going wrong right now. You can't think of anything can you? Because the only problem is you!"

"But you see, I am you. I am a part of you. *You* are the problem."

Tears rolled down my face again. I turned directly to her. "I can't DO this. I can't give you so much importance. You can't control my life. I need you to leave. I need you to go. Now."

Deepika 2.0 looked shocked, "You'll come right crawling back. I'm sure of it. You know why? Because you're pathetic!"

"Get out NOW!" I screamed, "I'm done with this, I'm done with you ruining every good moment in my life! If you don't leave NOW, I WILL!"

Deepika 2.0 got off my bed and opened the door to my bedroom. Right before she shut the door, she turned around and said "Hey, Deepi, I'm so proud of you. Don't forget your strength and I won't forget my humility," She shut the door.

I cried in relief! She was gone! She really was. I had done it! It had taken 16 years, but I had finally gotten Deepika 2.0 to leave me alone! In the past, the most I had gotten to was to get her off my bed, but she never left the room, never left me like she did today. I was sure that I would see her again, but I was also confident in my ability to stand my ground. This was progress. I was a work in progress. And that gave me hope.

I finished the meditation, texted Astrid, and went to sleep early, excited to see what growth tomorrow would bring.

my girl

my girl will be adored by the crowd
not for her looks but for her
strength.
her dedication.
she will not be afraid to go out in the night,
like i am.
my girl will stand up for herself—
in school, at work,
the way i hope i will.
no one will ever question her right to be where
    she is.
no one will undermine her talents.
they'll be just as proud of her as i am.
but i'll be the proudest,
for getting the privilege to say "she's my girl,"

mathematics

two negatives make a positive
huh?
it's easy to make light out of any situation isn't it?
with the excuse of this god forsaken phrase

two abusers make a positive?
because they don't know any different and
their kids are used to it.
used to wiping the tears of their mother
used to being embarrassed in public
used to wincing at the drop of a pin
it's their normal.
their "daily ritual."

so in a way,
two negatives *do* make a positive.
they make a never ending cycle of
unshaken children,
who never got the chance to cry,
and should have been too young to grow up.

A Mother's Intuition

I always thought that my first trip outside the country would be to some place exotic, with a significant other on my right arm, on some remote island, and a bottle of champagne in my left. What I got didn't involve champagne or a significant other, but hey, at least it involved an island. *England.* Not as exotic as I had hoped, but still just as exciting. Home to all of my favorite people: Freddie Mercury, David Bowie, Louis Tomlinson, Elton John, Hugh Grant, and of course the three Harrys: Prince Harry, Harry Potter, and Harry Styles. The list of people that I love who were born and raised in Britain goes on for ages. And on this trip, I was determined to meet someone famous. *Anyone.* As long as they had a British accent and a few thousand followers on Instagram, I'd be satisfied.

I had woken up a week before my 16th birthday with a neck ache. I wondered why, but then I looked under my pillow and found a hard cardboard birthday card. I looked inside to see the message, *To our love, happy birthday. Let's find you a prince for you to marry so that you'll get off our backs :) With love, Mom and Dad.* In the card were 4 plane tickets: one for my mom, my dad, my sister V, and me.

I screamed and jumped out of bed, "Mama! Dad! "Thankyousomuchiloveyousomuchyouguyshavemade-mylifeworthit,"

"Wren?" My mom walked out of the master bedroom rubbing her eyes. I ran up to her and squeezed her hard.

"Mom, thank you so much. You know how much this means to me and I can't thank you enough," I snuggled into her shoulder.

Looking half asleep, my dad managed to say, "Happy birthday darling," before I jumped on him.

"Ok ok enough talking, let's get packing!"

The trip over was smooth for a 12 hour flight. I kept thinking that I had forgotten something, and constantly forced the people next to me to move, so that I could check my bag, checking for every last thing. I was nervous because I'd never been on a plane ride for more than 2 hours, from San Jose to Los Angeles and back. Now, I was going so far, but it would all be worth it. I was going to be in my favorite country for an entire week, and I was going to make the most of it.

We landed at the airport, and as I stepped off the plane I smelled the misty aroma and took it in. This was England, baby.

I looked to my right. V was on her phone, mindlessly trying to find some wifi to connect to. I sighed, annoyed that she could never get off that stupid thing. V was my 13-year-old sister, and the only thing she was good for was hacking venue sites to get me the best concert seats.

She was in her annoying "I'm too cool for you" phase, but when she wasn't trying to be someone she wasn't, she was pretty fun to talk to.

I looked outside the windows of the airport and saw a flurry of beautiful white, something that I had never seen. It was snowing! Being from California and never stepping out of the state basically meant that I never thought I'd be able to witness anything but sunny weather and wearing thick sweaters and jackets any time the temperature was less than 65 degrees. But here I was, in the place known for a White Christmas: England.

As a family, we weren't very religious, but we always celebrated Christmas since my birthday was December 24th. We had landed on December 23, and I was determined to make the most of this time abroad.

"Look V, the snow!"

She rolled her eyes and didn't bother to look up. I looked away, pretending not to care, but out of the corner of my eye I saw her looking out the window, and smiling. *There she was.* The real V.

We got our bags and waited in the immigration line. I got called over.

"What's your name?"

"Wren Simpson,"

"What's the purpose of your visit?"

"To meet a famous Brit."

"Pardon?"

I blushed, "Sorry. I'm here on vacation for seven days with my mom, dad, and sister. We're celebrating my sixteenth birthday," I smiled.

The immigration officer looked at me and chuckled as he stamped my papers, "Well have a good birthday. Oh, and Happy Christmas."

"Merry Christmas," I replied, practically giddy.

I met V and my parents on the other side.

"So, what should we do first? Our hotel room isn't available till 4 p.m. You guys hungry?" my Dad asked.

"No," I said. I looked at the time. It was 1 p.m. We had a few hours.

"So Wren … This is your favorite place, and your birthday week. What do you want to do?"

"Three words. *Fortnum and Mason*."

Back at home, I was an avid tea drinker, on the brink of addiction. I truly believed that tea was not only a drink but an experience, and a 5-story store dedicated to selling that experience was the closest thing to heaven on Earth.

I forced my parents to let us ride in one of those authentic black British cabbies, which gave off the most vintage, authentic, British vibes. As we drove over, I put in my earbuds and played my "for when dreams come true" playlist, full of all my favorite songs by my favorite British artists. I looked out my window and saw the London Eye and nudged V. She smiled at me, and I smiled back, and I hugged her. I took out one of my earbuds.

"I'm so happy," I told her.

"So am I," she said.

I gave her one of my earbuds to share, and she obliged. *Asleep* by The Smiths was playing, and we both dozed off, extremely jet lagged.

Not long after, our mom woke us up. We had arrived. My dad paid the cabbie as I stood in awe of just how big the store was. I had seen pictures, but nothing could have prepared me for the real thing. I took V's hand and we ran in, with my parents screaming behind us, telling us to be careful. We entered to a packed floor full of sweets, and we both grabbed a cart and started piling in stuff. Turkish delight, scones, clotted cream and jelly, toffees. The list was endless.

A young, good looking guy came up to us and asked if we needed anything.

"Yes. Can I get your number?" I giggled.

V gasped. He politely said no, but it didn't hurt to ask. I was allowed to be outspoken here, in a country where no one knew who I was.

The interior itself was very sophisticated, with long staircases leading to each floor, and a beautiful crystal chandelier at the top. There were lots of Christmas decorations too, which helped with the ambiance the store was trying to create.

We met up with my parents who both looked surprised with the amount of stuff we had picked up. My dad started to say something, but my mom nudged him silent.

"Let them have fun," her eyes seemed to say.

We moved on to the next floor. *Tea.* Shelves and shelves of tea, all different types and flavors. It was a dream come true. I walked around the whole floor and decided to take a Christmas Calendar Advert, with 25 different teas. I took a deep breath through my nose and smelled the warm, spiced aroma of all the mixed teas. I looked over at my smiling parents, and I could see just how much this vacation was needed for everyone. We went to the fifth floor for fun, to see if they had an opening for high tea, but it was too late for that, and it had to be booked in advance. My mom made a booking for the 27th, and we went downstairs to pay for everything.

I looked over at V, "This is what I wanted to do. You can pick what we do next. It's your vacation too."

"Wren. You can be selfish just this once. I know how much you've been waiting for this. And I'm having fun," I gave her a disbelieving look. Who was this and what had she done to my sister? "I promise. Let's just have fun!"

"Ok then. I'm thinking that tomorrow we can go to Abbey Road Studios and take the iconic Beatles picture." V's eyes lit up. Our family bonded over our love of the Beatles. My father had proposed to mom with a (horrific) parody of "Hey Jude," and the rest was history.

We left the store with four bags, onc for each of us to carry. Over half of the stuff was sweet treats that I had picked out, which all had a close expiration date, but I was sure that wouldn't be a problem. We called a taxi (a regular one this time) and I took out my earbuds, handing one to V. I was so happy when she took it earlier that day. We used to listen to music together all the time but around two years ago V decided that she was too cool for my mix of 70s, 80s, and boy bands.

I played "Meet Me in the Hallway" by Harry Styles. *Two, three, four* … The guitar kicked in and V and I both swayed to the beat. I kept thinking about how Harry Styles could be 2 minutes away from where we were, or the fact that Paul McCartney could decide to re-record "Wonderful Christmas Time" at Abbey Road Studios tomorrow as we recreate his iconic photo, and just how possible it was to meet all the important people in my life.

Signs kept passing as we drove: Paddington Station, Piccadilly Circus, Hyde Park. We finally came to a stop near Hyde park, which looked barren, but still beautiful. Mom urged us towards a row of two-floor buildings, all uniform with white doors, and brick exterior. We stopped at the third one down, and she unlocked the mailbox with a pin. *No way,* I thought. The box opened and out came a set of keys, which she used to unlock the door. All four of us stood with our mouths open in surprise.

"Mom! How did you find this place?"

"It's Megan's. She's letting us use it because she's staying with her parents this year. You should thank her, she thought you'd want to stay somewhere authentic for your birthday."

The flat itself was perfect. Two rooms and a small kitchen with low ceilings, but nonetheless, quintessentially British. The floors were all black and white checkers, which added to the English charm.

"You and V are gonna have to share a room, but we'll let you choose which one."

We both decided on the master (of course) and quickly unpacked and undressed. I put on the rest of the playlist, hoping to amplify the charm of our situation. We hopped into the queen bed, and fell asleep to "Tiny Dancer" and "Dreams."

"Wren?" I was being shaken awake. I opened my eyes and saw V and my parents smiling. My mom had a cupcake in her hand with a candle stuck in the middle.

"Happy Birthday, Wren!" they said.

"I love you guys so much. I can already tell that this'll be the best birthday I'll ever have."

We talked for an hour or two about a bunch of random things, and then tried to go to sleep for a few extra hours.

"Wren?"

"Mmmm" I said, half asleep.

"You know I love you, right?"

I grinned, "Yes of course V, and I love you too. Now get some sleep, you're gonna want to be fresh for tomorrow."

I woke up at about six in the morning to start getting ready. I took a shower in the smallest bathroom (looks like everything is smaller in England) I'd ever been in and proceeded to straighten my hair. I had a weird mixture of curly and frizzy hair, so I always felt more confident when my hair was straight. I put on some mascara and lip gloss and started on my outfit.

I felt like doing something as *avant garde* as possible and the first thing that came to mind was mixing patterns. I played "Gypsy" by Fleetwood Mac to give me the confidence to wear this crazy outfit. Hearing Stevie Nicks tell me that my "face says freedom" was all the pushing I needed. I decided to wear my favorite horizontally striped blue shirt, my vertically striped white and grey jeans, and a large, oversized, checkered coat. To top it off. I put on my biggest hoops and said a prayer. I looked in the mirror. Was I looking like a clown? Yes. But I was also feeling surprisingly comfortable, so I decided not to change anything.

I packed my mini backpack with my lip gloss, phone, and a sharpie. I went into the kitchen and found a box of croissants in the pantry and ate one, waiting for the others to wake up.

At around 8:30, everyone was up and getting ready. I sat in the chair by the door, trying to not show how excited I was.

Everyone was finally ready at 9:30, and I stood up, giving V a proper view of my outfit.

"Wow," she said. "You look … interesting."

"You don't like it?" I teased.

"No no it's not that! You're looking very Sgt. Pepper. In a good way of course."

"I'll take that as a compliment."

We decided to walk, since it was only two miles away and we wanted to take in the scenery. I got a few weird stares from people, but other than that, it was a pleasant walk.

There was something about the air. It was so much colder than California, it was as if it cut the tension of all conversations. The air lent itself to the wonderful time we were having. I felt like the weather made it so much clearer to me, to V, to my parents, that we were on vacation. That, and how different the layout of everything was. We stopped at an art gallery on the way, and I had to walk down these narrow, creaky wooden steps to see the special exhibit. I found it interesting, just how different London and California were.

After a few other distractions, we finally reached the road. The road that meant so much to my family, the road showcased on one of the best albums of all time. There were only a few people taking pictures, since it was Christmas eve, and most people would be with their families, preparing for Christmas.

"We're really here," my dad said in awe.

All around the road were white plastered walls, with signatures, and statements from fans who had come before us. I took out my sharpie and handed it to sister V, for her to add her signature to the wall.

"It's a fool who plays it cool" –V

I took it back and wrote *"pretty face on a pretty neck" –Wren*, in hopes of coming back in ten years' time to see my signature still there, right next to V's.

I looked past the bars to see it standing in front of me. "Abbey Road Studios," the place where all my favorite songs were recorded, where all my favorite artists sang. I looked at the sign: *DO NOT ENTER WHEN RED.*

No way. The light was flashing red. Right here, right now, someone was making history. I smiled knowing that there was a high chance that someone I loved was 50 feet away from me.

We asked a nearby lady to take our picture as we strutted down the road. I took my shoes off, to be as Paul McCartney as possible, and we got it. Our own little memory of this iconic place.

We went to the gift store for good measure, and I got a replica of the sign *ROOM 2, DO NOT ENTER WHEN RED.*

For dinner, we decided to eat in Soho, in a fancy Italian restaurant which Mom had already reserved plenty in advance. They told our server that it was my birthday, and the whole restaurant erupted in the most cheerful (yet slightly aggressive) version of "Happy Birthday" I had ever witnessed.

But the day wasn't over. We decided to continue walking in the Soho neighborhood, to prevent such a perfect day from ending. I looked up at the sky, hoping to see stars, but what I got was even better. Stretching the entirety of the long street, were the lyrics to Bohemian Rhapsody, in big neon lettering. I smiled, knowing that I was in the birthplace of Freddie Mercury, and when I looked to the stars, I could almost see him smiling back at me. It really was a day for British music.

As we walked back to our flat, my mom held my hand and whispered something into my ear, "You will see someone famous. Trust me. When you want something with good intention, the universe gives it to you."

I smiled but took it with a grain of salt. I wasn't going to force my happiness to depend on if I met someone famous. There was always LA for that. This day was the best one I'd had in my entire life, and I didn't want to taint it.

"I love you guys! Thanks for an amazing birthday."

V and I crept into bed, and I hummed "Space Oddity," drifting into a peaceful slumber.

It was Christmas morning. We exchanged small gifts and said a prayer. V had gotten me guitar picks with the faces of all the boys from One Direction, and I had gotten her a Mac Miller T-Shirt.

It was a lazy day; Mom had gotten some groceries and decided to make a pizza from scratch. V, Dad, and I were sitting in the master bedroom as Mom finished cooking. We played cards. My dad lost terribly every time, but indulged our egos.

"My baby girls. When did you get so big? I remember when you fit in the palm of my hand," he said to V, who was premature. "And you Wren. You're sixteen! Practically an adult. You make me so proud to be your father."

We had an emotional group hug that was cut short by Mom calling us for lunch.

After finishing our pizza lunch extravaganza, my mom had the idea to walk to Buckingham Palace, and we all obliged. But when we got within half a mile of our destination, we were blocked by a crowd of people, all looking towards Buckingham. I saw people pointing at the main flag, which was hoisted all the way up. I gasped. Wanting to confirm my suspicions, I asked the woman next to me what was going on.

The woman explained with a delicious British accent, "Didn't you hear? The royal family didn't go to Sandringham House for the holidays this year. They're here in Buckingham Palace this Christmas! They're coming out on the balcony to make an appearance at 4:30."

It made sense why there were so many people outside on Christmas.

My mom tapped my shoulder, "See I told you. As a mom, it's my job to never lie to you," she smiled.

I smiled back, resting on her shoulder as I held V's hand. Royalty definitely counted as seeing someone famous. We were about to see the Queen for God's sake.

Trumpets were played and although they were so far away, we were able to see figures in the balcony, members of the Royal family, of course. I looked to my left and to my right. The people who mattered most to me were these three. I was more happy with them than I was with anyone else, including the Queen of England. This trip had really shown me that. I didn't need anyone else to make me happy. I had traveled all the way to realize that I had all I wanted right here, at my fingertips. When you have your father's love, your mother's intuition, and your sister's trust, there's nothing else worth having.

COVID-19: High School (not) the Musical

Day 1: *Hip hip hooray, I live to see another day.*

Confetti has been dropped, the disco ball is prepped and ready. Welcome to the party. This is the beginning of your new life. Your new norm. It's very exciting, not having to go to school. It's almost like a never ending summer vacation isn't it? Here in California, we've just gotten the good news that schools are off for the next three weeks.

Long story short, the school has erupted in cheers, no one cares about the midterm they have to take next week, and spirits are high. Like, *really high.* It's lunch time, we're too excited to eat. Instead we go around congratulating people whose exams are cancelled, and saying goodbye to people who we won't see for weeks.

I, for one, am over the moon. The math test I've been dreading has been cancelled, and now I get practically a month to chill and hang out with my friends at the mall and beach. *It's summer baby!*

I walk to the car, say bye to my friends, and promise to meet up in a few days. Things couldn't be better.

Day 3: *What do you mean shelter-in-place?*

It's almost like a never ending summer vacation, isn't it? Wrong. The government has issued shelter-in-place, meaning no going out, no meeting my friends, and no fun. What am I supposed to do if I can't go out? And now that there are no classes, what does anyone expect us to do? There's only so much TV that one can watch. This is cruel, absurd. Preposterous, if you ask me.

Week 3: *Extended S-I-P?! Now that's just cruel.*

You're telling me that I can't see my friends for at least another month? That school is basically up in the air, and it's up to us to learn? This isn't what I meant when I said I wanted a break. I'm scared, and I'm sad. I don't want this to be my new normal. I want things to go back to how they were, when people weren't so wary of your race and your identity. I want to go back to the California I know, where everyone has a decent shot, not one where others distance themselves from certain people based on skin tone. We are going backwards! If we're not in this together, then there's no point of being in it at all. This is not going to resolve naturally. It'll resolve with the hard work of everyone, working together to find a solution for *everyone*. This virus doesn't see race, financial standings, or religion. In a funny way, this virus is the great equalizer. We're just too stuck up to see that. Too ignorant to think it'll affect us. But I'd be lying if I said that I'm not sad that life can't go back to the way it was. But we *can* adapt, I'm sure of it.

Week 5: *We are so freaking selfish.*

I get a call from family members overseas, who are all doctors. They're scared for their lives. This is a pandemic, and here I am, mad because I can't go to the mall?? I'm in a beautiful home, with enough food to go around, and people who love me. Our mentality has to change, or else what we're doing is for nothing. And as humans, it's pretty clear that we hate when our time is wasted. So if you can't find it in the goodness of your heart to stay home for the safety of others, do it for yourself. And remember that we are not invincible, that after some time even the Earth gets sick of humans acting like we rule the world. We don't. We abuse it. And this time will show us all the things we can do to prevent that type of abuse from ever happening again. Today I vow to think bigger than myself, than *my* happiness. I'm in it for the long run, and you should be too. Will we remember this as a time where we sulked, or a time where we came together, and rose up? I'm hoping for the latter. This is our karma, and we have to ride it out, and remember our place. Only then can we move forward from this and expand into our full potential.

lucid dreams

october
the best month of the year
they wrote a song on it
"we fell in love in october"

i want a chance to have that
to have a chance at falling in love
did you know i was born in october?

i dream with a purpose
purpose to wake up in a world different from my own
to finally have a chance,
to be with *you*

because who knows how long it'll take
to be with you in real life

for weeks i try
and try and try
and then i think
maybe it's not worth it,

who cares about love anyway?

Author's note

Well, there you have it, a wide variety of different views on different topics, from a teenager's point of view. I hope you enjoy these stories and cherish it as I have. Take this book as a reminder that you can do anything that you put your mind to, if you just keep your end goal in sight.

Thank you to my parents for always pushing me and believing in me. Without your constant support this would have never materialized or flourished into what it has.

Thank you to my friends for always being there for me (you know who you are :)).

And finally, here's to you, the reader, and all the things that you're going to accomplish.

All the love, Kimaya <3

About the Author

Kimaya Saijpal is an Indian American teenager living in the San Francisco Bay Area. She is a mental health advocate and activist who spends her time educating teens on the power of meditation. She believes that meditation can change the frequency of the world to a higher vibration. In her free time she enjoys being a lead vocalist in a band, listening to music, writing, traveling to new places with her parents, and discussing the nuances of life with her close friends. For further information on the effects of meditation in a young adult's life, visit her website at www.kimayakalm.com. *Angst, Anxiety, and Acceptance* is Kimaya's first book.

CPSIA information can be obtained
at www.ICGtesting.com
Printed in the USA
BVHW060458110720
583375BV00005B/35/J

9 781614 310761